Not Just Me

Not Just Me

Julia Prosser

authorHOUSE®

AuthorHouse™
1663 Liberty Drive
Bloomington, IN 47403
www.authorhouse.com
Phone: 1-800-839-8640

© *2011 by Julia Prosser. All rights reserved.*

No part of this book may be reproduced, stored in a retrieval system, or transmitted by any means without the written permission of the author.

First published by AuthorHouse   09/09/2011

ISBN: 978-1-4670-3372-5 (sc)
ISBN: 978-1-4670-3371-8 (ebk)

Library of Congress Control Number: 2011916220

Printed in the United States of America

Any people depicted in stock imagery provided by Thinkstock are models, and such images are being used for illustrative purposes only.
Certain stock imagery © Thinkstock.

This book is printed on acid-free paper.

Because of the dynamic nature of the Internet, any web addresses or links contained in this book may have changed since publication and may no longer be valid. The views expressed in this work are solely those of the author and do not necessarily reflect the views of the publisher, and the publisher hereby disclaims any responsibility for them.

Diary Entry

I feel like I should just be better and all of this should go away. I am scared to death of what I am and more scared of what will be left of me. I am not me. Me who feels things I shouldn't, me who tries to reach out but can't, me who wants to be alone but can't stand actually being alone. The spontaneous urge to not be me, with no one else to be.

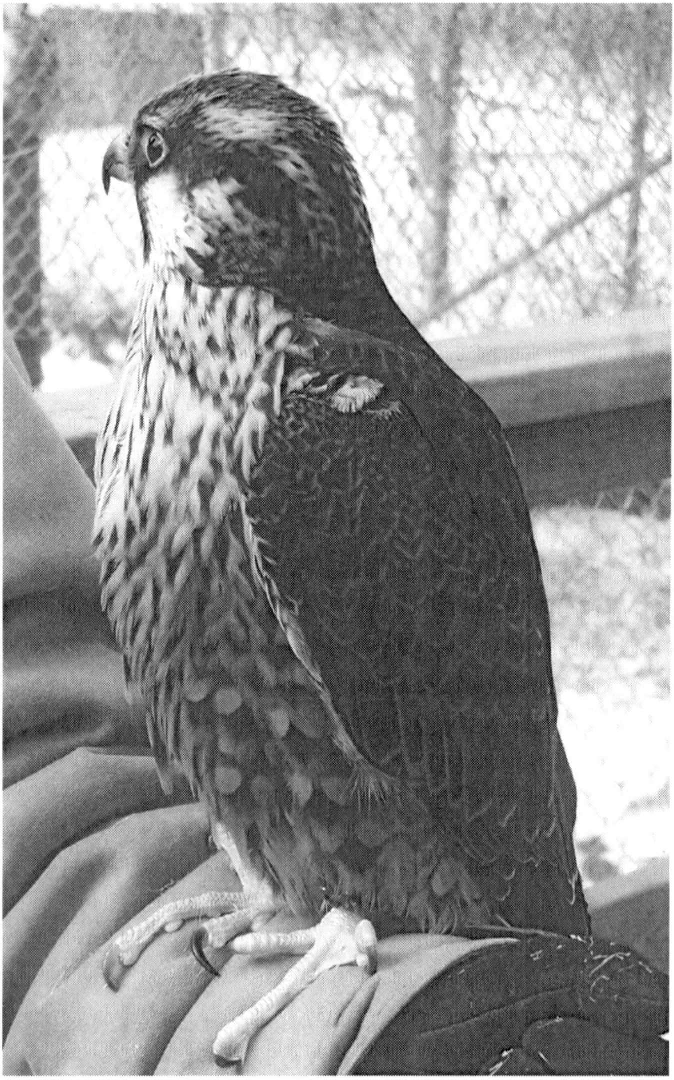

Freedom

You set me free
So how do you feel
Always looking after me
Can't hide from what's real

Tears fall down your face and mine
Emptiness fills my soul
So many feelings I can not define
Each of us playing a role

Friends forever but lovers no more
The kiss of true love in the past
Happiness was mine until fate closed the door
My fantasy to good to last

A bird with clipped wings can not fly away
It is bound to the ground with invisible chains
I am the bird, awaiting the day
For my wings to grow back so height I can gain

Fear

Lightening bolts shine
And thunder breaks
Saying I'm fine
As my heart aches

Your voice and touch
Are a stranger to me
Yet I care so much
Is it to good to be?

With the ground far away
I am floating and free
Will my trust be betrayed?
Will you run from me?

The answers draw near
But no comfort is found
With answers comes fear
And now I am bound

Bound to an illusion
That reality will take
Filled with confusion
With so much at stake

Silent Screams

Alone for so long
Can I change my ways?
Find where I belong
With someone who stays

When I was young
Life was so kind
To innocence I clung
Truth I would never find

With each passing year
With new lessons learned
I face my fears
Trying not to get burned

But trust has become
Something unknown
Opening up to some
When a reason in shown

So I sit on my bed
Thinking of youthful dreams
The reality that I dread
And my silent screams

Free

Vulnerable and free
I fly like a bird
Only now can I see
What before I only heard

A wall made of stone
Once covered my heart
I was always alone
Only playing my part

But the wall is now gone
My heart now exposed
My love for you is strong
This is the path that I chose

I long for a glance
Or a touch of your hand
A night when we dance
Or have nothing planned

My dreams are now reality
My knight in shining armor awaits
While I am here making my plea
It is my heart that he takes

Unwanted Answers

I felt my mind go hollow
My fingers and toes go numb
My mind or my heart should I follow
I thought I wanted answers to come

But the answers I sought are full of pain
My mind in this tug of war
I know that the love we feel is the same
Just not the same as before

"A day ahead
May come" he said
"When me and you
Are only two"

I waited for so long
But the day never came
I know we don't belong
And there is no one to blame

Loving Face

The stars shine bright
And moonlight calls
To see the light
As my heart falls

Alone in your truck
The music playing
The lightning that struck
With what you were saying

The look in your eyes
Your gentle touch
Then you replied
I care very much

I like what has started
And don't want it to end
When we have parted
I want to be friends

I kissed your lips
And held you tight
Loosing my grip
On what is right

You still want to see me
I long for your embrace
My heart being set free
With your loving face

Second Best

The moon shines bright
As it speaks to the stars
With it's magnificent light
I'm still behind bars

Your love set me free
Made me fly like a bird
Love and passion I could see
Without a single word

Your eyes told your story
That you could not tell
You did everything for me
I knew you so well

But the knowledge I had
Didn't save me from this
For you left me behind
With one final kiss

Love made me blind
For all the signs were there
New love you did find
But I know that you care

Our days together are done
This has been my test
For so long I was number one
Now I'm just second best

Caring

It starts again
No signs to tell
Will it never end
This trip through hell

The warmth of your touch
Set my heart free
The thought was to much
Still to blind to see

Ice turns to water
From hell fire's heat
My thoughts I do ponder
A never ending feat

Still left alone
While your sitting there
Fighting fantasies of my own
That you really could care

Forbidden Love

Alone in the hallway
You held me in your arms
The high price we pay
To let down our guard

You said I was the one
You'd waited for all your life
But with that night done
My mind fills with strife

Were the words you spoke true?
For they explain how I feel
The feelings were not new
And with a kiss they were sealed

But my feelings are forbidden
For another you do love
So my feelings must stay hidden
In the gloomy clouds above

Never Ending Fight

So alone and in the dark
Emptiness fills me completely
My fingers go numb, my stomach sick
Why is this happening to me?

The rain fell down in streams
But in your arms I was safe
The crystal drops didn't seem so bad
They seemed to fall into place

Your arms still protect me
Yes, I know this is true
But darker thoughts appear
When I'm not protected by you

Your kiss is still as sweet
As any candy found
Love passes through your lips
A love that is now unbound

To hold you tight and say goodnight
I have to start letting go
But as I hear your heartbeat race
The warm winds start to blow

The wind warms my heart
For another rainy night
Gives me the strength that I need
For this never ending fight

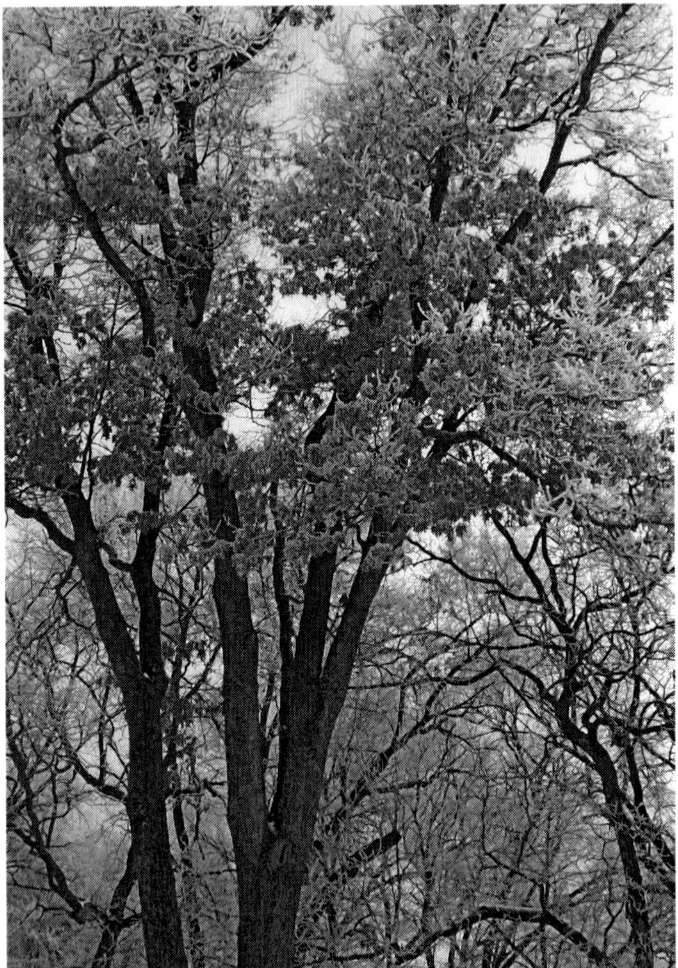

For You To Know

I was in the forest today
Walking through the snow
Thinking of all the things I would say
So my feelings you would know

I can't stop thinking about you
My heart aches to feel you near
I honestly don't know what to do
My own true feelings I fear

I think of all the things you've done
The love that was in your eyes
The warmth that remained when your lips were gone
After you pulled your mouth from mine

My feelings I never admitted to you
Because you showed no signs to tell
I know just what your going through
But I'm going through my own hell

I don't know if I will hold you again
Or ever feel your touch
For your heart isn't mine in the end
But I know that you care very much

Wedding Day

Down the Isle I walk
In a white flowing gown
Our gazes locked
I then look down

Rose petals are scattered
Leading the way
My dreams once so tattered
Are coming true today

Your smiling face
Is like a dream
As I take my place
The tears start to stream

With a lift of your hand
And a soft caring touch
I now understand
Why I love you so much

Our lives we now share
So many dreams to come true
With the ring that I wear
And the words "I do"

Funeral

Down the isle I walk
In a black silk gown
My gaze is locked
I then look down

Flowers and bows
Leading the way
Dreams only you know
Crash down today

Your emotionless face
Is like a dream
As I take my place
The tears start to stream

With a lift of his hand
And a soft caring touch
Our son understands
Why I love you so much

My life I will live
But I wait for the day
When my life I can give
So in your arms I can stay

Crash

Is it too much to ask
To want you near
An impossible task
Finding a love that is dear

Hold me close
And kiss my lips
Let me impose
A lover's bliss

But do not seek
What I can not find
For I am too meek
And you are too kind

Reality's life
Is a love that is lost
Or a day of strife
With a friendship tossed

But reality isn't gone
It's the dream I live
For I am a pawn
Reality's life I will give

For the hurt doesn't show
When reality lies
It's when the dreams I know
Crash down that I die

Day Dreams

A soft caress
A caring look
True feelings expressed
That I mistook

I thought it was romance
Beginning to bloom
But there was no chance
Unless it's in your room

There was no caring
Just heated desire
No future for sharing
All destroyed in the fire

You walked away
No words to explain
For the rest of my days
I'll live with this pain

No thoughts of my future
No thoughts of my past
Just one more daydream
To good to last

Chaos

To go through life
Alone and free
To watch other's strife
But never really see

Or to see the pain
Of the ones you love
But always restrain
So you watch from above

To finally be happy
Do you need to be hurt
Learn to feel empathy
Before you find your heart

When you finally learn to feel
And find your heart denied
You've given away that sacred shield
That before you used to hide

It is very hard to see
Where true happiness lies
In the deception of our dreams
Or the chaos of our lives

Like a Dream

We revealed what we feel
Now and in the past
Our friendship sealed
Can our relationship last?

To feel your arms surround me
Pulling me to your chest
Knowing what can not be
Doing what is best

I asked about last night
That seemed just like a dream
The feelings that we fight
Nothing is how it seems

To push you away, again and again
It's something I have to do
To be friends alone, we must pretend
Not showing our feelings so true

The kiss I long for
Never to be mine
Things not like before
For now I'm not blind

A Marine

You had to leave and go far away
To follow your heart, besides what could we say

You took a stand, did what is right
For our honor and trust, now you do fight

Your family and friends, we all stayed behind
A life to call your own, I know you will find

To walk on the beach with your toes in the sand
Not sure of exactly what destiny has planned

But when night comes around, look into the sky
You'll see all of us waving, not a wave of good-bye

But saying we miss you, and wish you were here
And we think of you often, although sometimes with tears

Things will work out, you'll come back in the end
For it's here you have waiting, many true friends

You will return with knowledge of what you have seen
For now you are more than a man, you are a marine

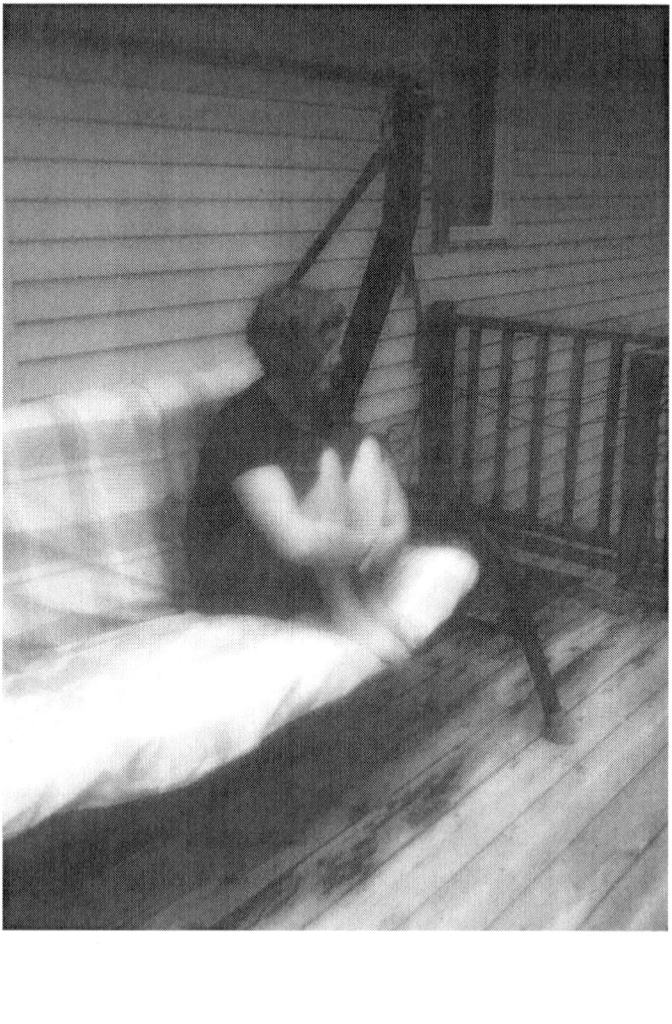

Friends

I sit alone
As others draw near
Though friendships have grown
Nobody cares

Wrapped in their own worlds
Which their loved ones share
And watch mine unfurl
Knowing life isn't fair

I then look around
I'm surrounded by friends
But no comfort is found
For my heart will not mend

Because nobody sees
My heartache inside
I'm down on my knees
But they are all blind

I am there for them all
But they are not for me
For the farther I fall
The more they don't see

Diary Entry

Just the pain to be alive . . . to deny the urge to be other than that. Change hair color, cut you hair, cut it all off, rip it out, anything. Make me not me. Please voices that are my own and yet not my own. Death without death. Thoughts moving to fast but I don't know what they are. Can't sit still and yet frozen. Agitated, numb. Falling down the rabbit hole. Things are hazy, unreal. Who knows? No one.

Disappeared

The leaves turn colors, then they fall
The cold wind blows, my heart he calls

He calls to me, he cries my name
The friendship grows to a lovers flame

Without a touch I feel him near
And with his words, I face my fears

Hand in hand we deal with strife
Together we stand, confronting life

I then awake, and find I'm alone
Not knowing why, for no reason was shown

You just disappeared without a trace
No sad good-byes or last embrace

Diary Entry

I only see the faceless person in the mirror. Why is she here. What does it all mean? She wants to take me over. She is my darker unnamed, the one who comes out when I go numb, or need to fool others that I am normal.
NORMAL—what is that?

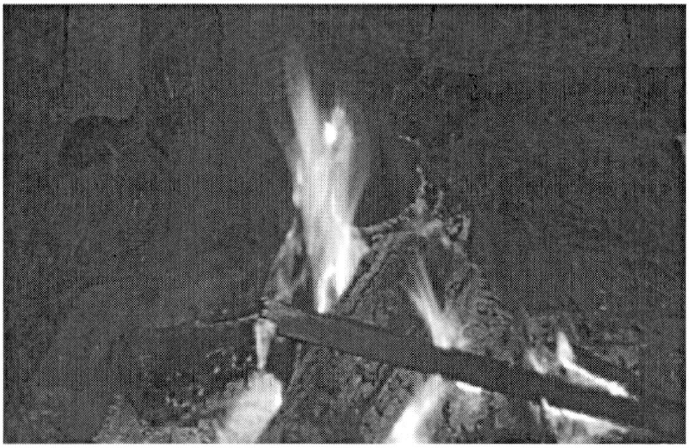

Dying Heart

What is life?
Is it just a cruel joke?
A double edged knife
To a heart that is broke?

What is love?
Is it freedom or chains?
Do you fly high above
Or drown with the pain?

To a heart that is bound
Love is a fire
Consuming the ground
So your feet float higher

To a heart that is free
Love is a weight
Pulling you down to your knees
Screaming at fate

I can't help but wonder
What force decides
Which hearts grow fonder
And which ones die

Love Lost

I look around
But no one is here
No one hears a sound
As I shed my tears

My heart feels hollow
My energy drained
I try not to wallow
But each smile strains

Why is life so cruel
So unforgiving and mean
A cold storm brews
An unmerciful dream

Is love the answer
Or is it the cause
My mind starts to stir
As I think of loves lost

Diary Entry

It is amazing that what is seemingly important at one point is so not important. Only bad memories are what I have, resentments and regret. Yes I regret my time with him although I don't regret much else in my life. The unicorn does not regret anything. I am so much like the unicorn. At least I like to think I am. That is why I think I will always be alone. A solitary creature who touches many people's lives, but can never be truly obtained.

Diary Entry

Oh well, that's all you can do I suppose. Admit it. At least I can be me and not have to pretend I am someone I am not. I think most people do that, put on false faces to people to make them seem acceptable. Maybe not a false face, just not true to themselves.

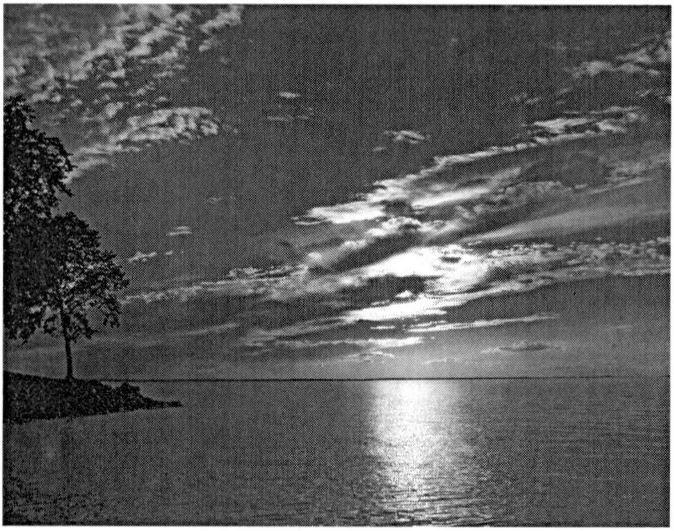

Bird's Song

The beautiful lake
Sun shining down
With so much at stake
Now, with love found

You have not phoned
Or stopped by to talk
I feel so alone
The door is now locked

I feel so unsure
Of how to react
When I should stir
You can't take words back

You say that you love me
How can I believe?
My heart says it can be
That you won't leave

But experience has shown
The heart is often wrong
For once the bird has flown
It changes it's song

Wonderful Life

A spark of life
Rays of sun pouring down
To become your wife
In a white flowing gown

A dream I live
In shining armor he waits
Our hearts we give
With no more constraints

The dream slips away
A coldness surrounds me
I awake to the day
And a cold reality

A day without love
Is a day full of strife
But when I see the stars above
I lead a wonderful life

Passing By

If I place my trust in you
You will turn and walk away
Leaving me feeling blue
With nothing else to say

If I expect you to leave
I won't be caught off guard
Although I know that I will grieve
It won't be quite as hard

I know it's not fair
But life rarely is
To find someone who cares
Is a fantasy's bliss

That is how I see life
I know I may be wrong
But with days filled with strife
The feelings are very strong

If while hiding from my pain
Life is passing me by
I will see what remains
With few tears that I cry

Diary Entry

Am I ready for a relationship? I don't know. It would be nice, but I am unstable. Still on a high wire without a net. The winds have died down a bit, but . . . always a but, who knows what will happen. I am medicated and sort of numb, taking it all in but not processing it at all. On the edge just waiting for the stress to push me over. Into where? What is below this edge I am at? Deep depression, being high as a kite? A combination of both? I also fear the panic attacks that happen every so often. It is almost like I have no control of what I do when that happens. It is as if my mind leaves my body. I drove home from my sister's house and don't remember the trip. I was having a hard time breathing and felt like I was going to throw up. I started sweating and yet felt cold. My head spins, thoughts race and I can't keep track of them. I feel like a complete failure.

Lasting Love

Each second that I share with you
Means everything to me
Our love will last a lifetime through
For it was meant to be

My feelings that you describe as drear
Are not the ones that are true
They are the ones that come with fear
That I might be loosing you

I try to find the words to say
Exactly how I feel
But I know your love will find a way
To tell you what is real

I never want to be the one
Who hurts you deep inside
I want to help you see the sun
My love will be the guide

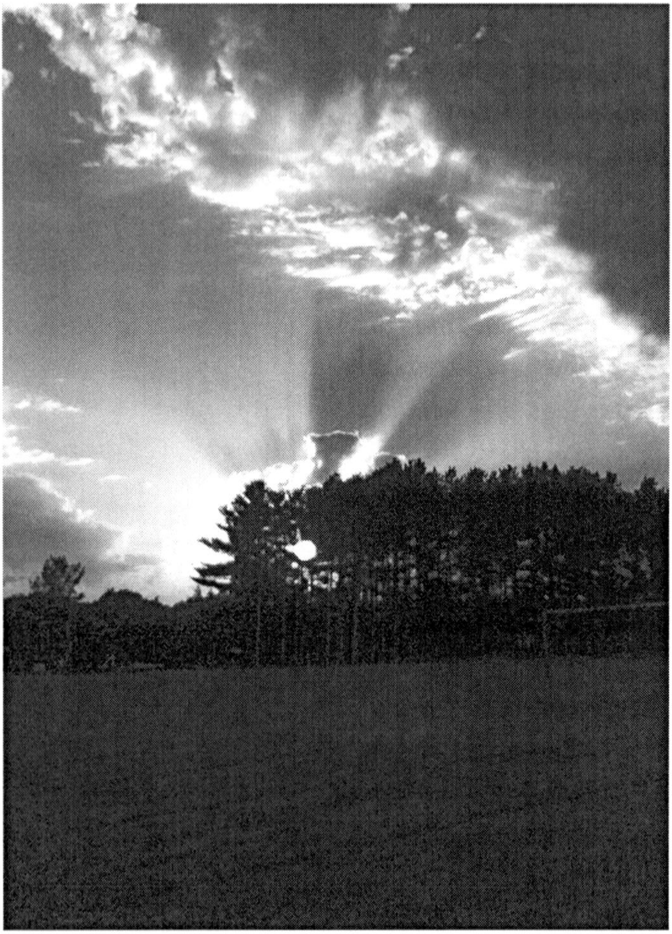

New Hope

Grey is the sky
Black is my heart
I started to cry
As my world fell apart

My first love I lost
I live with that scar
I pay the cost
When they go to far

No one understands
The world that I live
They have only one plan
To see how much I'll give

Then you walked in
With a warm and strong embrace
And a new day begins
With new hope I can't erase

Hopes and fears fill my heart
Awaiting a sign from you
Don't make my world fall apart
Show me your feelings so true

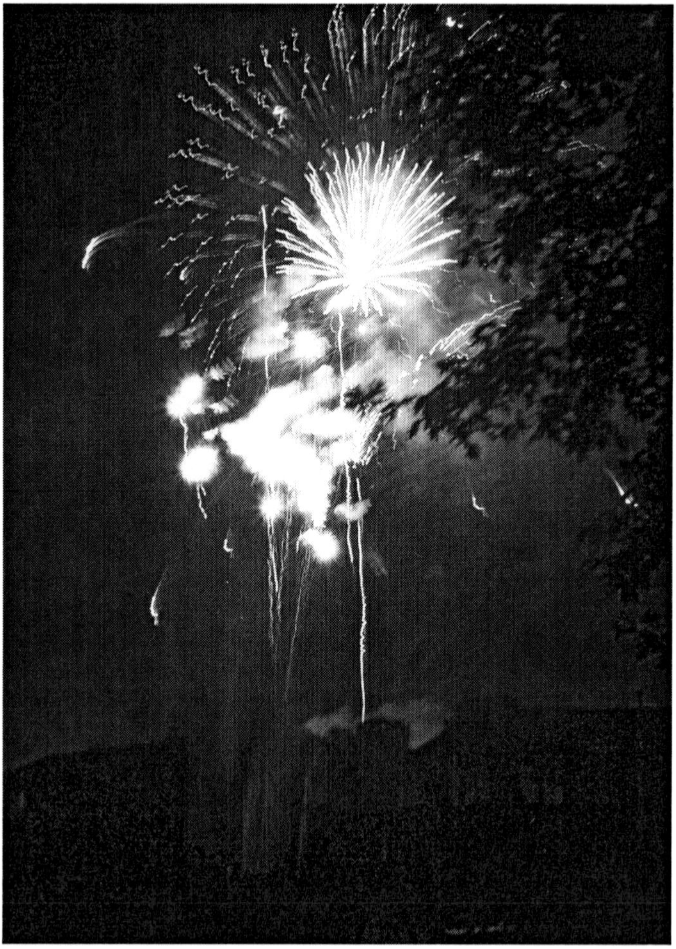

Illusions

No matter what the dream I live
Or the wishes that I make
No matter what I'm willing to give
My illusions reality will take

Whether it's a slap to my face
Or a knife placed in my heart
Love and happiness will find no place
In a world that has fallen apart

I'm reminded in the end
That life is never fair
No matter how much I pretend
Fate is not one to care

So if it's happiness that you seek
Love that you think we could share
Look to the stars, when you speak
The ones who decide live there

Diary Entry

Reality—Something that I hate to include myself in. I much prefer my version of; they think of me often but all of their phones are disconnected so they can't call me, or I was a missed opportunity so they can't bring themselves to face it and that is why they haven't called. Or, maybe they all realized how out of their league I am and are all to embarrassed to call. But, **cold hard reality,** I am just not missed.

Lost fantasy

Alone in the dark
The stars on my wall
To open my heart
When destiny calls

Emptiness fills me
My mind goes astray
My days all seem dreary
With words you don't say

My fantasy is lost
While searching for truth
How high is the cost
When losing your youth

With my feet on the ground
Ignorance is life
No answers are found
For days filled with strife

Diary Entry

I haven't had a drink in quite a long time and would like to have a couple of drinks tonight. I just want a night when I can not be sober and just forget about everything in life. Bottoms up.

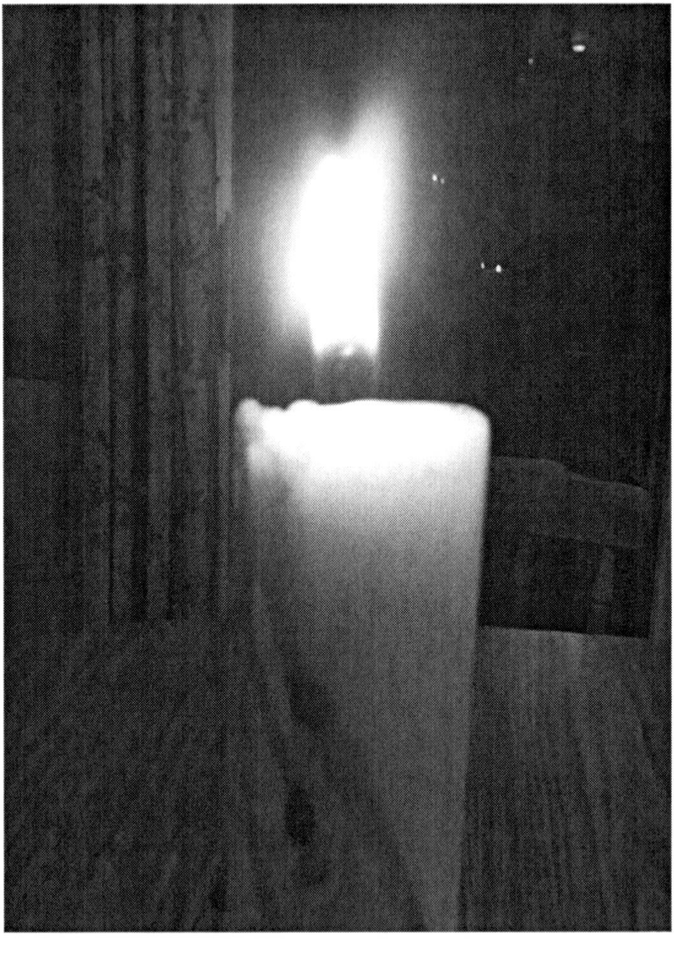

Bleeding Soul

Candle light shines
Perfume I can smell
Peace I can find
While I'm living in hell

The water covers my soul
It makes my blood run hot
My heart is paying the toll
To find the love it has sought

To have it once before
But sit back and watch it go free
My heart is now at war
No one more scared than me

Let go of old love
And trust someone new
I wish I could fly like a dove
Into a sky that's always blue

Fly away from deceit
Lies, pain, and shame
Wounds to deep to treat
With no one to blame

Not sure of what I want
Not sure of what I need
My heart he haunts
My soul left to bleed

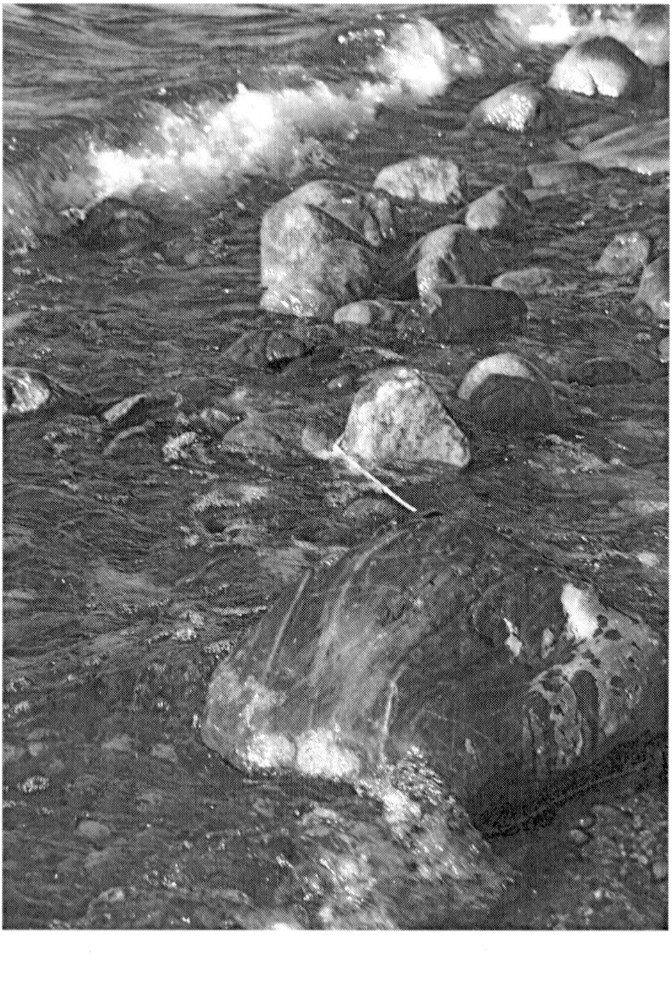

My Drug

It runs in my veins
They say it gives me life
Through all of my pains
My life is but strife

My head feels light
My stomach hollow
While making my plight
My problems I swallow

The rush then takes hold
My heart beating faster
To break trust once told
Would be a disaster

Control is then lost
My mild goes astray
With all my troubles tossed
Into a sky that's so gray

With violent convulsions
My own type of drug
The feeling of repulsion
Through hell and back I'm tugged

To start all over
Each and every day
My fight to be sober
Isn't going away

Diary Entry

I am starting to feel agitated and fidgety. I don't know why I feel like this. It is almost like something very violent takes hold of me and throws me around. My fingers ache and my mind starts to whirl. I feel like I want to throw everything around. Take hold of the coffee table and toss it, whip it, overturn mirrors. Anything that will relieve me of this, this feeling. It's like I am crawling out of my own skin.

Bonds

I sit and ponder
About last night
Was it wrong I wonder
Even though it felt right

Wrapped in your arms
With my heart beating fast
I let down my guard
Is it a dream that won't last

We will talk soon
But what will you say
That your feelings are true
Or will you walk away?

The best of friends
We've been for so long
Although everything ends
Even bonds that are strong

Final Good-Bye

To not hear your voice
And not feel your touch
You made a choice
Still I care very much

You said that you care
And wanted me near
As my fragile web tears
I live out my fears

To be a part of your life
Living from day to day
For now days filled with strife
With games that you play

No time is spent
And you don't seem to care
The rules you have bent
And now they aren't fair

I think about you a lot
Then I wonder why
The lessons you taught
End in a final good-bye

Trust

I trusted you
Believed what you said
A stupid thing to do
I should follow my head

The heart misleads
And sadness it brings
On life it feeds
Draining bite that stings

If something is wrong
Just let me know
If we don't belong
Or feelings don't show

But talk to me
Don't leave me to hang
Your heart is free
But spare me that pain

My Dreams

Always alone, as others draw near
Of all things, being alone is what I fear

A change of pace, do what is best
But no love is found, to my unrest

People think they know where I stand
But the life that I lead, is not what I planned

Will I ever find someone who holds me close
A love that binds us heart and soul

Someone who looks beyond the outside
And sees the passionate heart that I hide

Sees my loneliness, my pain, my fears
Who loves me still and kisses away my tears

I will never find this person it seems
For he lives only in my dreams

Love's Knife

The sun shines bright
While fields of clouds seem to fly
Stars come with the fall of night
As I remember our good-bye

I remember the kiss
And holding you near
Both things I will miss
As memories appear

I see birds flying around the trees
Spreading their wings out wide
Everything around them sees
Their beauty, grace, and pride

As I return to my life
I know one thing to be true
My heart was cut out with love's knife
And left behind with you

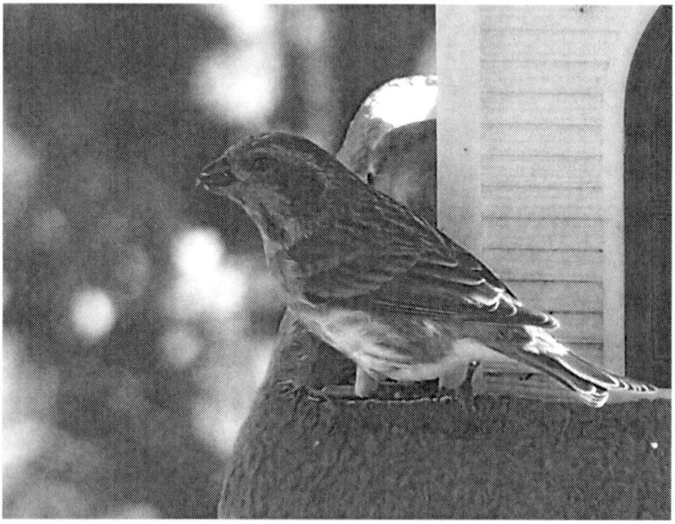

Immortal Fame

No one who cared
But everyone's death
I just sat there and stared
Not even one breath

To obtain immortal youth
You left us behind
Searching for the truth
We will never find

The deepest of sleeps
Was yours to take hold
Through memories we keep
We try to be bold

Move on with our days
With no one to blame
Though everyone pays
For your immortal fame

Diary Entry

I know how horrible I have felt and I know the pain of death being more promising than life.

Distance

Open up and see
What you have missed
Open up to me
Learn to take a risk

I know you've been hurt
But hiding hurts you
Open your heart to the world
Show your feelings so true

But the world doesn't care
And here I am safe
Although many do stare
They all keep their space

Any pain that I feel
Self isolation has caused
Although just as real
There is not as much lost

So please understand
If I seem distant toward you
It's not what I planned
It's just something I do

No One Who Cares

Betray my best friend
And follow my heart
Stick it through to the end
As her world falls apart

I know he loves her
But is his love true?
Inside his heart stirs
Outside a storm brews

If he loves her as he should
To make her his wife
Then he wouldn't have stood
Confessing his mind filled with strife

I will stand by his side
Through whatever road he takes
His heart will be his guide
In the choices that he makes

So if she is to be his wife
I will be standing there
Wondering why no one in my life
Will show me that they care

Thanksgiving

Be thankful for what you have
That is always what I hear
Grabbing food during the half
Of the football game each year

"Turkey Day" is another name
Bringing the focus to the food
With the "How are we going to carve the turkey?" game
The entertainment is always good

People say it's a joyful time
But what does this day mean to me?
It means I get away from the daily grind
And spend time with my family

It gives me a chance to tell them all
How much they brighten my life
And when I forget to call
They have never left my mind

So peace and love while we are apart
My loving family
Those by blood, and others by heart
For you are the world to me

The Last Good-Bye

The last good-bye
On what seems a normal day
The tears you cry
As they take him away

The words left unspoken
Haunt your heart and soul
The bond that was broken
Left in your heart a hole

Everybody comes to you
And gives you a hand to hold
Though nobody knows what your going through
You feel that you must be bold

You try to move on
With all your days colored gray
You try to belong
Does the pain go away?

The Myth

I live a life
That no one sees
Each day filled with strife
That no one believes

Or maybe they know
But just don't care
They say it's not so
For that wouldn't be fair

A life without love
Is no life at all
I watch from above
As others fall

Fall into a life
They are comfortable with
To become someone's wife
Is no longer a myth

The myth is mine
To enjoy and hate
For life is not kind
And neither is fate

Childhood Rhymes

Whatever happened to fairy tales, boy meets girl, they fall in love, live happily ever after.

What happens when boy meets girl, they fall in love, but that's not enough . . . disaster.

Knight in shining armor, fighting for his honor.

Someone on the street corner, begging for a dollar.

Wizards with crystal balls, magical horses with wings.

Unbelieving, self centered people. Politicians pulling our strings.

Castles with towers, dragons guarding treasure.

People hurting others for their own pleasure.

I wanted to live the fairy tail life but that was stolen with time.

So I am stuck in this world, escaping only with childhood rhymes.

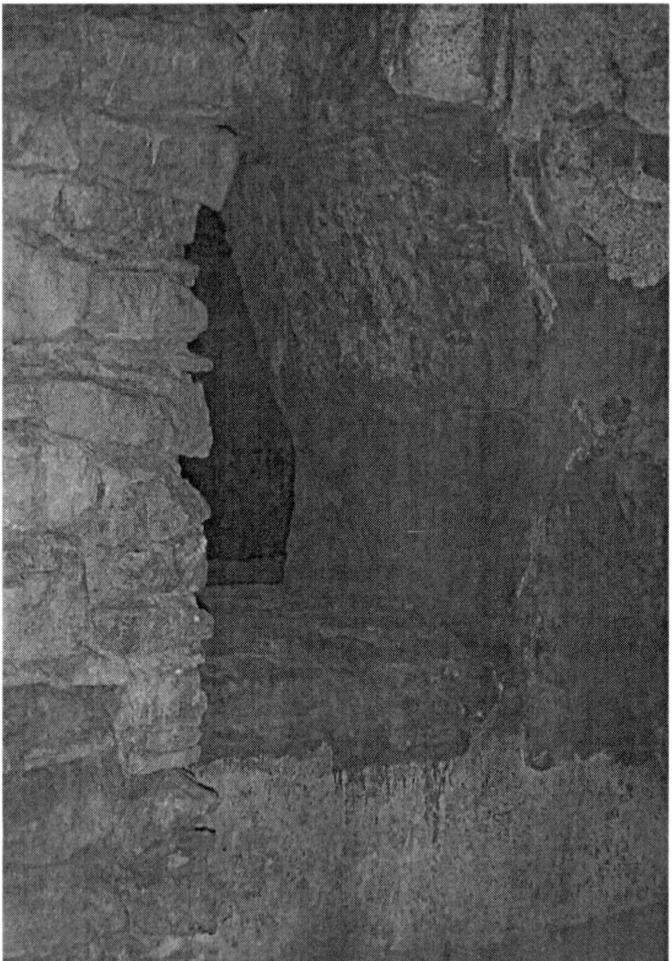

Madness

To wander about
A limitless sky
To take a different route
By saying goodbye

To flitter around
On fairy's wings
To never be bound
By reality's strings

To walk on a cloud
While time stands still
To be alone in a crowd
By your own will

To hear the calls
Of a voiceless man
To walk through walls
By knowing you can

To fit in every day
With the ones you hold dear
To push them away
By embracing your fears

Diary Entry

Once you know you've been crazy you fear madness of many sorts. Everything falls into categories; depression, manic, hypo-manic, what is normal? A state to which I don't remember. Do I have too much energy? Not enough?

A True Friend

A true friend to talk to
Who will always be there
And when I feel blue
I know that you care

The words that we write
And the things that we say
Make the skies seem bright
Even when they are gray

To my problems you listen
Without a complaint
As my teardrops glisten
You think I'm a saint

No matter what happens
Disappointment doesn't show
For we know in the end
That friendship still grows

So my trust I have placed
Into a friend that's so true
Recalling many things I've faced
Because I had you

Never Bad

Love forbidden
Yet still burning strong
Feelings were hidden
For so very long

I watch love grow
From a friendship's flame
Once you were low
But your feelings were the same

The love of your life
Is not who it seems
The days filled with strife
Caught up in your dreams

Confusing and sad
As life sometimes is
Love is never bad
With true love's kiss

Signs

I have to believe
Fate is pointing me this way
That I should retreat
While others stay

The lack of interest
That you have shown
The point that you rest
While others go on

These feelings I denied
For far to long
No longer can I hide
I have to be strong

Something out of the ordinary
Or so it seemed
A strange piece of stationery
With someone's dreams

Dreams that conflict
With my own
They contradict
What I was shown

The love that I thought
Would guide me through
Has lessons it taught
From the storms that brewed

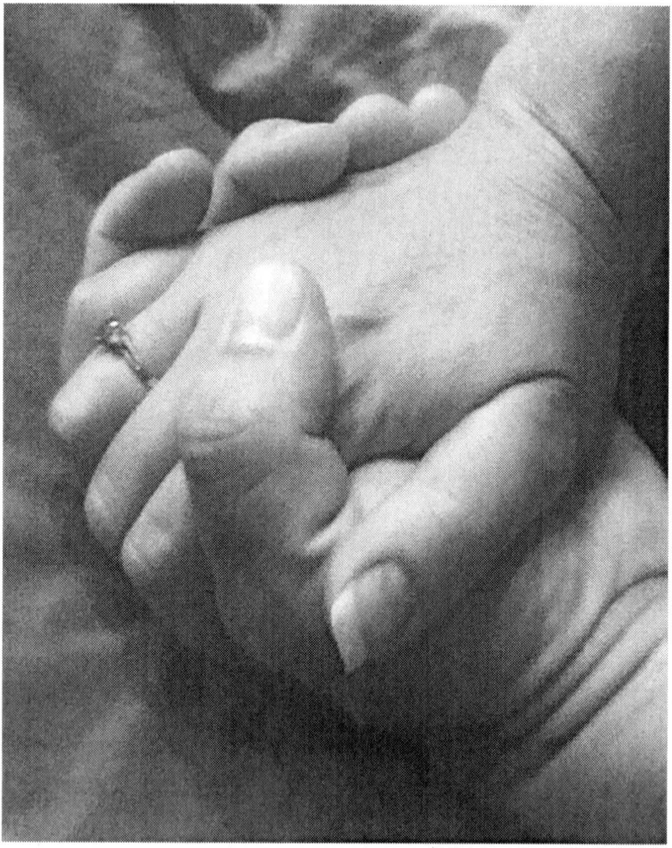

Real Love

I have found my destiny
The love I can say is real
You have set my heart free
And I know exactly how I feel

You will always be here
With your loving smile
My heart has vanished any fear
And is no longer in denial

With all of my heart
My love is forever yours
We are never apart
For it's you my heart adores

Because you are you
Nothing less and nothing more
My love will always burn true
A lifetime of love is in store

Stranded

It seems as though
I now cause only pain
Confusion grows
Should I stay away?

I was so sure
Not that long ago
But even feelings this pure
Are sometimes not so

It is not what's intended
But I feel the hurt
I feel a bit stranded
Because you have my heart

Maybe I am wrong
And just thinking to much
For our love is strong
My soul you have touched

Falling

Everything around me falls
My life is coming to an end
I can't control who my heart calls
And I have lost my best friend

You broke down the wall around me
And changed my view of life
But there was something I refused to see
And that something was your wife

You told me that it was over
And that you needed me near
But that was just a cover
For I am facing my biggest fear

The reality of life, without true love
The reality I used to know
Although we were chosen from stars above
It takes effort to make it grow

The effort was too much this time
Even though you are the one
There is no fault, no blame, no crime
I just have to face that we're done

Middle Ground

Over react, or don't speak my mind
I wish there was middle ground I could find

I know you are doing the best that you can
And I am doing my best to understand

As much as I love you, and know you love me
That love is blinding, makes it harder to see

For that place in your life, I held in the start
It's no longer there, it has fallen apart

Or maybe it was never really there
A thought then, and even now, I can't bare

For a life without love, is a life without you
Though I have loved before, this love is true

Fate won't hide forever, simple signs are shown
Some a bit bolder, after others go unknown

Hidden Words

I made a mistake
And asked how you feel
The part of me you take
The rest left unreal

You say that you care
But are worried about future times
And that life isn't fair
Like love is a crime

I don't understand
What it is that you want
It's not what I planned
But my heart you do haunt

The words are unspoken
But distance you've placed
My heart you have broken
With memories erased

So just let me know
What you're feeling inside
The feelings you show
And the words that you hide

Tormented Soul

I saw your face
When I walked in the door
Your eyes held no trace
Of the love that's no more

I turned around
And walked away
I didn't hear a sound
Though you were screaming my name

Any love I had felt
Vanished with the sight
As the two of you melt
My feelings seem trite

My heart has been lost
I once felt so whole
But my love you have tossed
Now see my tormented soul

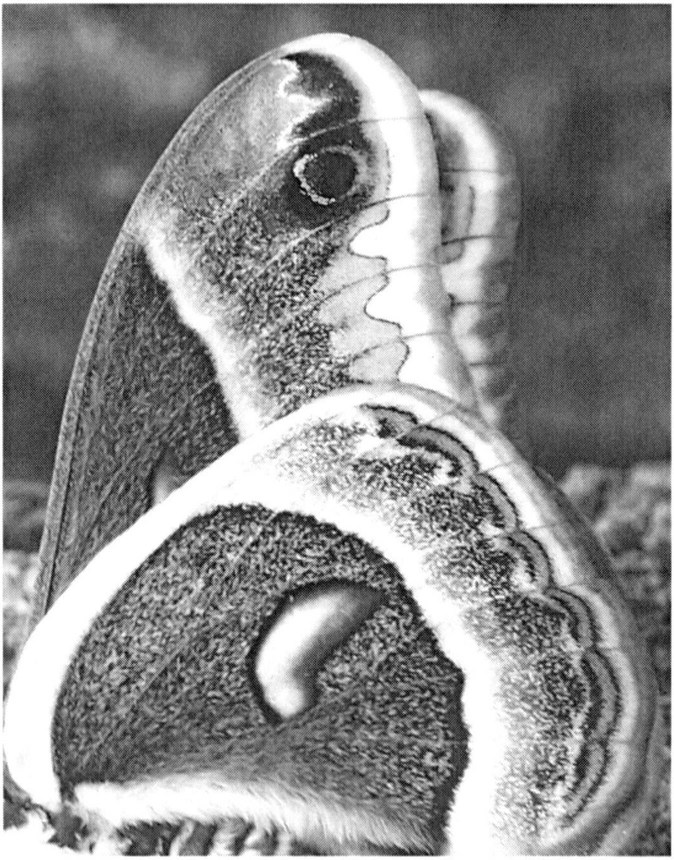

The Butterfly

Surrounded by love
Yet still all alone
From the blue sky above
The butterfly is born

From pain and darkness
She brings joy and light
Feelings one harnessed
Are now in full flight

With wonder and grace
She flies through the air
When she finds the right place
She can show that she cares

But despair and deception
Are not far behind
Her own false perception
Brings love she won't find

Her wings are now tattered
No longer feeling rage
Even though she was battered
She made her own cage

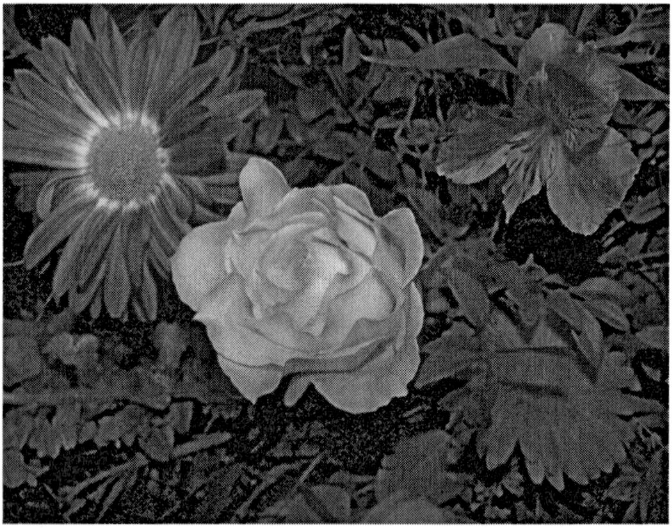

The Garden

A new door opens
To a life of dreams
While the old life ends
Sounding sorrowful screams

Longing for the pleasure
Of a lovers bliss
Knowing to treasure
Each and every kiss

This garden is new
Yet familiar in time
With love it grew
Flowers once left behind

Only small shadowed fears
Survive with the sun
With your love holding clear
The darkness that comes

As I look into your eyes
I now can truly see
Like someone who is wise
How true love can be

My Crime

To feel pain so deep
To feel joy to intense
To feel sadness and weep
To hurdle it's fence

Then thunder sounds
When there shouldn't be
Nature isn't bound
So why are we?

Bound to emotions
We can not define
Some spiritual notion
That somehow confines

Confines what we feel
And when we cry
Confines what is real
Reality defined

I refuse to see
And feel what others do
Feeling is to me
Overwhelming and cruel

So most of the time
There is no pain, joy, or sorrow
Only my crime
Of a numb tomorrow

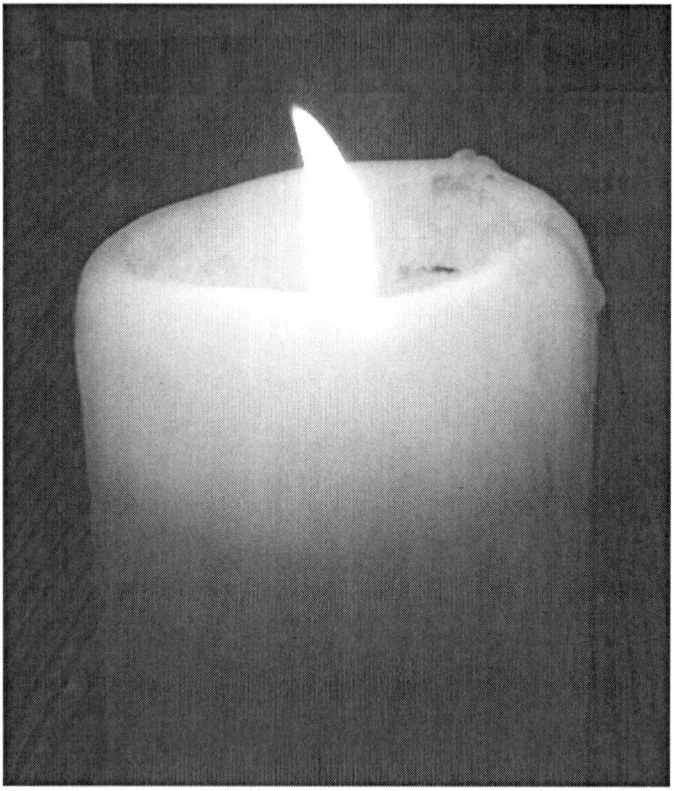

Darkness

The candle light dances
It flickers and flows
Caught in the enchantment
No one else knows

A strange voice calls
Was it imagined or real
Reality sometimes falls
Into that darkness I feel

This darkness causes
My hardships and pain
It feeds on the despair
With no need to restrain

I turn back to this flame
Dancing and swaying about
There is one thing that is a shame
It always gets snuffed out

Spoken Words

If words are spoken
Will they change life's path?
For a situation can exist
Even if it's not stated

If words are spoken
Will everything get better?
Or maybe get worse
Some things should never be said

If words are spoken
Will I change?
Become someone new
Someone I have tried so hard to deny

If words are spoken
Will I stay the same?
Live in denial forever
Leading a life that I hate

If words are spoken
Life will be real
Feelings labeled
And I will have to feel the pain

If words are spoken
I realize the pain is real
And will never go away
If words are not spoken

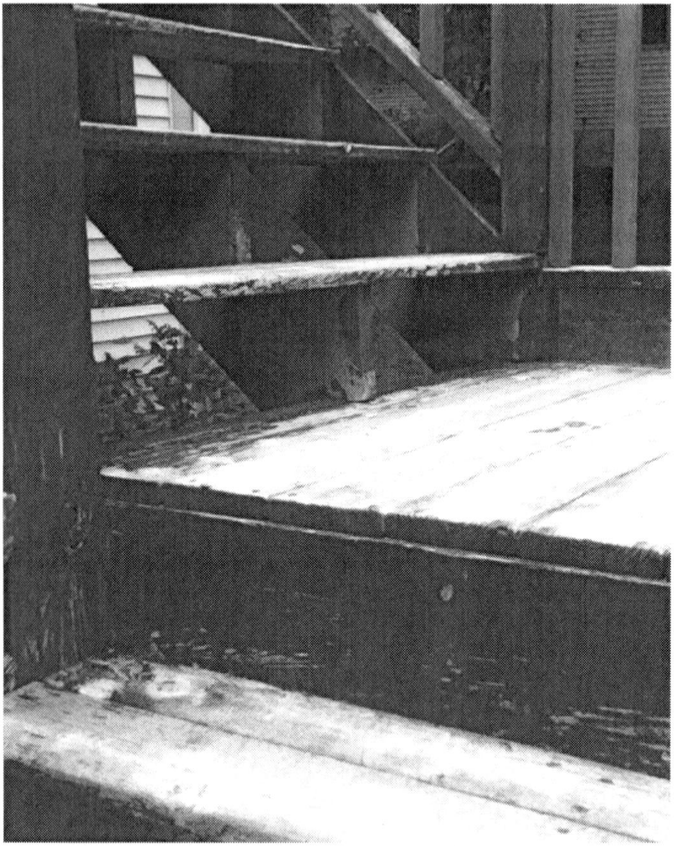

Steps

They say it's the first that is the hardest to make
I think it depends on how many you take

Think of a hill, steep and large
The decision to climb it may be hard

But isn't it later when you feel the burn
All alone, half way up, with no one concerned

The decision was made, so everyone forgets
Bur the pressures and pain never relents

Some give up and roll down the hill
Others struggle on as their soul the trip kills

Some say it's the first that is the hardest to make
I think it depends on how many you take

Diary Entry

Courage is very important with all of life's steps. I mean sometimes you have no choice but to take the steps, or there is little room for error. The line is very thin and shaky. Sometimes you weakest moments are also your strongest. I mean when I was at my lowest and decided, with some assistance, that I needed help. I had crossed that line and needed help to get back. I told my sister that I felt weak for being me basically and she told me that I was the strongest person she could think of.

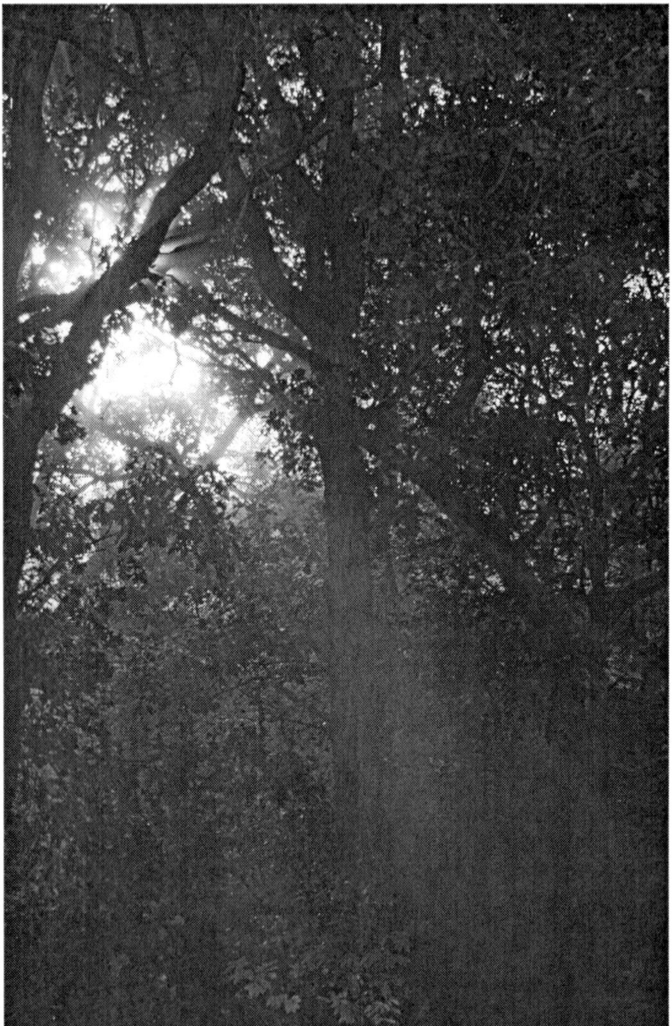

Shadows

You stand in the darkness
Fog surrounds you . . .
Rolling, moving, twisting
Eerie silence echoes
Frozen in fear you dare not move but shadows move around you, encircling you.
The moon is full making every tree haunted.
"Is this a dream?" you think.
It seems real, you can smell the wet grass beneath your feet even though you can't see it.
Something brushes past you as you hear a loud "CRACK" behind you.
Heart pounding you slowly turn around . . .
You see the face of a trusted friend and relief washes over you.
He beckons you toward him.
As you get close, you see the blade which he plunges into your heart.
Lying there limp and bleeding, the last sound you hear is him saying

"I love you"
                      Then laughter.